ARIS

TO

PRAYER

MEN OUGHT ALWAYS TO PRAY...

BY

DAVIDSON UTSAGHAN

PUBLISHED BY

KRATOS PUBLISHER

ARISE TO PRAYER

Copyright ©2023 by DAVIDSON UTSAGHAN

Published by: Kratos Publisher

CONTENT

INTRODUCTION

We see that the lifestyle of Jesus Christ was a life of prayer whilst He was on earth. The Bible says in Luke 3:21

(Luk 3:21) Now when all the people were baptised, it came to pass, that Jesus also being baptised, and praying, the heaven was opened,

(Luk 3:22) And the Holy Ghost descended in a bodily shape like a dove upon him, and a voice came from heaven, which said, Thou art my beloved Son; in thee, I am well pleased.

Evidently, his life of prayer led to the heavens being opened; he was a prayerful man. We, as believers, must understand that prayer is a necessity.

(Luk 6:12) And it came to pass in those days, that he went out into a mountain to pray, and continued all night in prayer to God.

We can see from the scripture above that Jesus prayed all through the night till the morning. So prayer is mandatory for every believer. We are seeing the emergence of the Daniel Generation that will pray and they are not afraid (Daniel 6:10-28).

And also a rise of Sceva's generation from Acts 19: 13-17.

(Act 19:13) Then certain of the vagabond Jews, exorcists, took upon them to call over them which had evil spirits the name of the Lord Jesus, saying, We adjure you by Jesus whom Paul preacheth.

(Act 19:14) And there were seven sons of *one* Sceva, a Jew, *and* chief of the priests, which did so.

(Act 19:15) And the evil spirit answered and said, Jesus I know, and Paul I know; but who are ye?

(Act 19:16) And the man in whom the evil spirit was leaped on them, and overcame them, and prevailed against them, so that they fled out of that house naked and wounded.

(Act 19:17) And this was known to all the Jews and Greeks also dwelling at Ephesus, and fear fell on them all, and the name of the Lord Jesus was magnified.

They wanted to manifest the power but did not understand the mystery of the secret place, for the power they sought was in the place of prayer and intimacy with God. They, however, tried to use the names of others for authority; we can see that in our generation, with people praying in the name of the God of their fathers or even the name of the God of their spiritual fathers.

When this is the case, the area we have manifestly failed is in the reality that there is an absence of the secret place and prayer life of intimacy with God. Whilst these spiritual fathers being mentioned operated from the place of prayer as a priest. To the next generation, they operate like a car without the engine. As it is revealed in scripture through looking at the sons of Sceva, they were sons of the chief of the priest. The name Sceva means mind reader, so even though they could size people up and read their minds, they did not have the power that comes from the place of prayer, and they did not know God intimately.

"Prayer is a power source, nor a power bank. So plug in! "

This is similar to our generation, where everyone is pursuing the popular, crowd and clout, yet there is no glory nor cloud experience. We can not pursue a crowd that is without a cloud. The cloud symbolises the presence; nothing will show up if we pursue so many platforms. God is calling us back to the place of prayer. The demon in the story of the sons of Sceva said; Paul, I know, Jesus, I Know, but who are you? Because Paul was a man in the place of prayer and intimacy. The same Paul among the fellow brethren challenged them with the saying "I pray in tongues more than you all". (1cor 14), we can conclude that Paul prayed like never before! Paul was a man who was knocked down from the horse by Christ and put into the Secret Place for three days and nights (Acts 9:9). The demon said Jesus I know, this means Jesus was a man of prayer, and the Bible records more than 25 times the prayer and prayer-life of Jesus. So for believers, prayer is mandatory for our future and daily lives on earth, it is like food for us and must be a lifestyle we live.

"Prayer is not a ritual, It's a culture of the saints."

When we pray, we make tremendous power available for operation, and hell begins to know who we are.

A command begins to rise inside of us. A prayerful person will always walk in power and dominion. I say again that God is calling us back to the place of prayer; the Lord Jesus said that my house shall be called a house of prayer for all nations (John 4). Today we see the church with so much fun, fleshy and craziness. Whilst I have no problem with disco lights, and smoke machines in the church, what good is it if all the light in the church is artificial, yet no power manifests within the church? So much smoke yet no glory cloud? Demons are harbouring our homes, churches and lives, and it is time for a generation that can pray to rise up!

PRAYER IS SPIRIT
WHEN PRAYER IS BIGGER THAN YOUR ROOM

In Genesis, we see man conversating with God, and in our time, God wants to take us back to Genesis, where the man was having a conversation with God which is what we call prayer (Genesis 3:8-9). Prayer is intercourse where we speak with God directly, and we are not using another medium such as stone, or building but a direct spiritual conversation. Prayer is spirit because God is omnipresent and omniscient!

(Matthew 28:20) Teaching them to observe all things whatsoever I have commanded you: and,

lo, I am with you always, *even* unto the end of the world. Amen.

It requires faith, so prayer is a spiritual reality. We know from the Scriptures that God is Spirit, so a conversation with him cannot be from a fleshly perspective. Therefore, we can say prayer is not flesh, but prayer operates on the spiritual level.

"Prayer is not powerful in your room only, it can be powerful everywhere – don't confine it".

Our heads represent a spiritual dimension of prayer as well as our bellies. Prayer goes from the head to the belly, which means that it goes from our thoughts to our spirit. In the head, you have your eyes and ears where distractions frequently occur, however until prayer moves from your head to your belly, there will be no expression of the spirit.

The Bible says (John 7:38) that out of our bellies shall flow rivers of living waters, which means that when we move from our heads to our bellies in prayer, a transition occurs from the earthly into the heavenly dimension. When we pray, faith is the engaging factor that must transport our requests to God. Faith is spirit, fake is flesh. When we pray, we pray by faith!

(Heb 11:1) Now faith is the substance of things hoped for, the evidence of things not seen.

(Heb 11:2) For by it the elders obtained a good report.

We can see from the scripture above that obtaining grace comes when faith is in operation. This is made active through prayer. So when we, through faith which is spirit, commune with God, who is spirit, there is a spirit-to-spirit connection that leads to fruit on the earth. Just like the fruit of the spirit is in the spiritual dimension, we can see it's the manifestation in the natural through our character in the natural. In the same way, prayer by faith manifests in the earthly dimension with active results. Prayer is a communication between God and man. It is a dialogue with divinity, giving divine access, prevailing in human efforts. So you can pray at work, park, church and whilst you are driving. The power of prayer is not in the length of prayer; although the length of prayer gives us good prayer discipline, the true key to prayer is not in longevity but in heart posture.

"Prayer is a relationship, it's not just longevity. Long is not Love!"

We must realise that God is raising us and calling believers back into prayers. Prayer must be in faith and humility; as we pray, we see and hear the fathers heart. Here is a definition I give for prayer, an acronym.

P - presenting

   R - request

     A - always

       Y – yet

         E – engaging the

           R – responsibility to see it

(Philppians 4:6) do not be anxious about anything, but in everything by prayer and supplication with thanksgiving, let your requests be made known to God.

So **P**resenting your **R**equest **A**lways **Y**et **E**ngaging the **R**esponsibility to see it. When we pray, we engage, which is faith in action; we pray, and heaven infiltrates this dimension; we engage the things we pray for and see the fruit. The power of prayer is in engaging. The power of prayer is that we now engage after we have presented our request. The above scripture says not to be anxious about anything, which means anxiety tries to overcome and override us.

We must bring it and table it with all supplication and thanksgiving; make your request known to God.

We, as believers, must understand the power of effective prayer. As we can see from James 5:16

(Jas 5:16) Therefore, confess your sins to one another and pray for one another, that you may be healed. The prayer of a righteous person has great power as it is working.

"Prayer is a heart posture, it is not a lip thing"

Other translations say the heartfelt prayer of a righteous person, which means the prayers must be felt in the heart. For effective prayer to be active, it must spring forth from the heart.

The scripture also says;

(Psa 66:18) If I regard iniquity in my heart, the Lord will not hear *me:*

Effectual and fervent in the Greek concordance means: To be Active.

That means active prayer, so prayer must be active and operative. It is, therefore, time for us to bring heartfelt prayers before the Lord and examine our hearts. For prayer is not about loudness or longevity but the posture of our hearts. God also says, in scripture, I, the Lord, search the intent of the heart.

Jeremiah 17:10 (NLT)

But I, the LORD, search all hearts and examine secret motives. I give all people their due rewards, according to what their actions deserve."

GUIDANCE AND PROCEDURES

God is our Father, and when we present our case before him, we must do so with the right attitude of mind to see effective breakthroughs. Prayers have rules and protocols, more like guidance according to the heart of the Father. It is more akin to guidelines and procedures, not rules per se. For example, our hearts must be clean, forgive those who have sinned against us, and be thankful. When the disciples asked Jesus and said to teach them how to pray, Jesus said to start by saying our Father who art in heaven, these are guidelines for prayer. Saying Our Father puts us in a worship position, where we lay down before Him, Crying out; Hallowed be thy name, a worship posture, a place of surrender. Thy Kingdom come, brings us to a place where he invades our realm with His mind. the word Kingdom in the Greek dictionary means Basileia, which is another kingdom or sovereign reign and rule (King + dom). He has come to colonise our minds and agenda, bringing his authority to take charge. When we say your Kingdom come to him, we say, God, we want your posture to shape us. Thy will be done on earth as it is in heaven, whilst we consider the earth in this prayer to be the global earth; in this instance, I want you to consider it as your life. You were made from sand, the soil of the earth, so pray as your will is being done in heaven; let it be done in me as a sign of the earth as one made from the earth. Give us this day our daily bread and forgive us our trespasses.

"The Principals of forgive before you approach is a must when praying"

So we can see the guidelines and procedures in play even in the Lord's prayer. We can't just stumble out of bed and say, 'give me God!'. I am sure, as a parent, your children can't just come into your room in the morning without saying good morning and beginning their request. If they did, there should be a rebuke or correction. In the same way, there are procedures and protocols with our Father in heaven. So God is calling us into the place of prayer. Prayer is a necessity for everybody. We must have a 'wordfulness' in us; what I mean is that the word of God must be full in our hearts and bodies. You cannot pray above the word level; if you do, it won't be effective in dealing with circumstances like altars or other complex spiritual matters. You must have a certain level of the word of God to pray effectively and prevail. The Father in these times is awakening the church back into the place where Prayer leads the church to intimacy with Him and also an upper room experience. I believe we are in the greatest awakening of His power and Prayer revival, the mantle of prayer Is coming back to the body of Christ and the Houses of prayer will be raised in these times. Revival is sweeping the earth again, prayers hubs where men will seek the face of God all night. I tell you this truth, if you can pray, you can prevail; God is looking for those who will sustain in the place of prayer. The devil's work in our times is to make us busybodies, where we run out of position, but if you can pray, you can prevail and stand the test of time. You will break through because all the solutions we need are in the place of prayer, and you will see the hand of God advancing in prayer. Years ago, I began to seek the face of God about something quite specific in my life. It caused a shift in my life because I was expecting a miracle from God, which led me to an intense season of prayer like never before. For a nearly whole year, God began to pull me into another dimension of prayer, so I prayed continually as God enabled me. For almost a whole year, I fasted and stayed on my knees, often seeking the face of God. In that period of time, I had an assurance that it would come, the job was not in place, yet I was a student, and I got weary and tired, so all I had to rely on was God in the place of prayer. God will only cause us to pray like never before if we are willing to posture ourselves. The more I prayed about this circumstance, the more God gave me assurance, and in a while, there was a breakthrough. Please understand this whatever matter you bring before God is not difficult for him. I have seen witches quit and people with demons surrender themselves and give their lives to God because of a human who can pray. If you are tired of the circumstances in your family, it is time for you to command on your knees and from the secret place. It is time to cause activation and command systems to shift. People often want to see a shift outwardly but yet do not want to travail and prevail inwardly in the closet. To be prevailing Christians and see the prevailing grace outwardly, we must first see it inwardly. Power shifts from the inside to the outside and not the other way around.

"Prayer Changes things you know and the things unseen for the now and future".

You can see that displayed in the upper room, Jesus Christ knew the power of the secret place. He sent the disciples to the place of prayer and told them to tarry ye in Jerusalem (the secret place) until they are endued with power from high. It was from the secret place they prevailed, and it caused people on the outside to wonder who these people were.

THE ELIJAH

GENERATION

Saints, God is calling us back to prevail
again! The ones that will crouch between
their knees until they see the manifestation
of God's promises (1 Kings 18:42-46). If you
can pray, you can prevail and stand
because a prevailing person is a travailing
person. You cannot tell me you have
prevailed without the travail; the place of
travailing is the secret place. Travailing
does not occur amongst the crowd but in
the secret place, so if you can pray, you can
prevail. God is causing men like Elijah to

rise up; Elijah was a man who prayed earnestly.

(James 5:17-18) Elijah was a man with a nature like ours, and he prayed earnestly that it would not rain; and it did not rain on the land for three years and six months. [18] And he prayed again, and the heaven gave rain, and the earth produced its fruit.

" Those who contend on their knees births divinity results into the reality of men"

I believe there is an Elijah Grace God is releasing in these times. Many people pray and invoke the God of Elijah and say Send down fire, oh Lord. However, they are not willing to adopt the prayer posture of Elijah. So we know that Elijah understood the technology of Prayer, he knew Prayer is spirit and faith is spirit and was able to have intercourse with God, who is spirit and therefore, God sent the rain. The mighty rain was birthed out of the posture of prayer. Do you notice that he sent Ahab, the king, to go and eat while he crushed his face between his knees and prayed for the rain until God answered? God is raising a group of people in this time that will walk as Elijah walked. So I pray that the Elijah anointing will rest upon us. It was prayer that forced the hand of the clouds to birth.

He understood posture and power, which caused his request to come to pass. Until you understand posture in the spirit, you cannot bring the interference of heaven to manifest on earth. The manifestation of Elijah's anointing is men and women praying as Elijah prayed. We also know that Elijah confronted the false prophets on mount Carmel (1 king 17). Elijah confronted in prayer. It is important to understand that before you confront physically, you must have confronted whilst on your knees in prayer. I have heard of stories where demons destroy people, and people have gone to confront spiritual opposition without first doing so in prayer on their knees. Until you confront it on your knees, you cannot confront it face to face. Every altar you try to confront on the outside must first be brought into the secret place with the Lord.

"Until you confront it on your knees, you cannot confront it face to face".

Gideon was a good example of this, as he brought the fleece before God and brought several things into the secret place before he went out to confront the enemy (Read Judges 6:12-28 for Gideon's experience).

There was certainly an altar erected in the heart of Gideon to the point that he became a living altar for God and could confront the altars of his father's house. He was able to confront because he got his assurance in the secret place. No one was there when God called him a man of valour. God validated him; many people are getting validated out there but not in the secret place. The fire is coming upon a generation and a people who will not give up. An Elijah mantle is being released at this time.

WATCHERS AND INTERCESSORS

When we understand that prayer is necessary, we will begin to see intercessors awaken back to their posts. Sadly in our time, intercessors have been abandoning their posts and pursuing microphones. Your strength comes from your knees, not the mic. Intercessors are supposed to be gatekeepers, but unfortunately, they have left their gates open. If you are reading this book and God has called you as an intercessor for your family or local city and you have been distracted by trying to expand into a global ministry, social media, and fame. Please wake up to reality! You cannot be contending against global adversities and warfare when you have not dealt with your local or family strongholds. David showed his Curriculum Vitae (CV) to King Saul of killing the lions and bears (I Samuels 17:36) before contending against Goliath. Let's stop playing, Intercession is bigger than mic shows. I am saying it's time to rise up in this time. God says in scripture, that he sought a man. Isaiah 59 says.

(Isa 59:16) And he saw that there was no man, and wondered that there was no intercessor: therefore his arm brought

salvation unto him; and his righteousness, it sustained him.

(Isa 59:17) For he put on righteousness as a breastplate, and an helmet of salvation upon his head; and he put on the garments of vengeance for clothing, and was clad with zeal as a cloke.

(Isa 59:18) According to their deeds, accordingly he will repay, fury to his adversaries, recompence to his enemies; to the islands he will repay recompence.

(Eze 33:6) But if the watchman see the sword come, and blow not the trumpet, and the people be not warned; if the sword come, *and take any person from among them, he is taken away in his iniquity; but his blood will I require at the watchman's hand.*

(Eze 33:7) So thou, O son of man, I have set thee a watchman unto the house of Israel; therefore thou shalt hear the word at my mouth, and warn them from me.

The watchers are by the gate, and if they keep it open, the devil and his systems will begin to interfere. Leaving the gates open is one of the fundamental things we must begin to address as we consider prayer and intercession; through their intercession, intercessors can stand and bring protection in the place of prayer. Many of the families of men and women of God have been destroyed because intercessors have been asleep. When was the last time the father woke you up at night, and you slept through? When was the last time the father woke you and you went to the fridge, and you thought it was craving, and you opened the fridge and after you ate? Whatever you ate, you went back to sleep. If this has happened to you, then you could have allowed critical situations the Lord wanted to entrust to you to skip through your hands. When last did the father put somebody in your spirit, and you became so ignorant? Not standing in the place of intercession when God has put someone in your spirit to pray for can lead to them being attacked by demons, sicknesses or even death. When God calls you as an intercessor to take a stand, you don't need validation from anybody. Stand in the place of prayer; stand in the place of power. To whom much is given, much is required. God has called us to intercede; the word intercede sounds like "enter and see"! It's a call to enter matters, by divine guidance. Looking at this in Webster's definition means *"to try to help settle an argument or disagreement between 2 or more people or groups to speak to someone to defend or help another person"*.

It means to intervene between two parties. So as an intercessor, you are mediating and standing in the gap. In scripture, in 1 king 3:16-38, two mothers stood before Solomon, contending for a child.

The heart of intercession was revealed in the mother when she asked for the child to live, whilst the one without the heart of intercession and whom was not the mother lied and requested for the child to be killed. The true mother was willing to give up her child. She knew it was not about her; intercessors know that intercession is not about them but the Father's business, the ways of God, and the will of God. Intercessors know that there is a groan in their belly, there is a place called the intercessor's groan, and there is weeping within them to see change happen, and the Kingdom of heaven come to earth. The Bible speak concerning Jesus Christ, our chief intercessor, our mediator, and intercede for us. The Holy Spirit is an intercessor too. So we understand that intercessors carry a groan in their belly. So, I call it intercessors groan; it is when the stress is addressed from the spirit realm. There is that groan in them backed by the Spirit realm, and when the spirit is in command, the intercessor's groan begins for a push for heaven's agenda on earth. There is a longing, a cry in their belly for a shift of something. Only if we can pray, only if we can be an intercessor again; For our family, for our territory. What happened is that we began to leave the posture. We see our cities, and we sense things coming in; a true intercessor will stand between the door and begin to cry out for the city unto God, we want to see a shift.

Our city will not be in ruin if we have men and women who can still pray. So God is calling the intercessors again. I love the intercessors' groan because we must understand that when the process of travail is in operation, there is that groan in them that begin to call them to arise. There is that place between the taking and the birthing, a place of uncommon travail. A sound within you is about to be released, and the devil is afraid, for that is the belly experience that causes you to pray, yearn and be restless. The Belly dimension represents life, seed and baby.

(Joh 7:38) He that believeth on me, as the scripture hath said, out of his belly shall flow rivers of living water.

So as God is calling the intercessor, we must begin to open up our mouths and begin to declare and release life. Hannah carried a child in her belly. There was a groan until the child manifested physically. After being mocked by the other wife, Peninah, she groaned before the Lord until the spiritual dimension of the baby manifested physically. She prayed until she forced heaven to bring the baby. So every believer must understand that God is calling us to intercession and prayers.

Here is another Acronym for prayer

P – Presentation

R - Reasoning

A - Above

Y - Young Hearted

E – Expectation

R – Remembrance

Presentation

(James 4:3) Ye ask, and receive not, because ye ask amiss, that ye may consume *it* upon your lusts.

Presentation is a necessity for us, and our hearts must be holy; the Bible says we must present ourselves as holy before him. Prayer is the presentation of the heart with holiness.

"Praying is not about shouting, but posture and willingness unto Christ".

So when we come into a place, before we bind, destroy, and cast every other spirit, we must check if we're living in the right place.

Reasoning

(Isaiah 1:18) Come now, and let us reason together, saith the LORD: though your sins be as scarlet, they shall be as white as snow; though they be red like crimson, they shall be as wool.

The reasoning factor of prayer is conversation. There is that place of conversation knowing that when you're speaking with God, give him time also to speak to you because often people say they are not hearing; God knows because you are not listening. So when we speak, if you are only the communicator, you are not having a conversation. You are just speaking and speaking. But so when we have communication, He speaks. It takes the dimension of maturity to receive mature revelation, therefore bringing everything to the place of reasoning and conversation.

Above

(Ephesians 1:21) Far above all principality, and power, and might, and dominion, and every name that is named, not only in this world, but also in that which is to come:

(Ephesians 1:22) And hath put all *things* under his feet, and gave him *to be* the head over all *things* to the church,

(Ephesians 1:23) Which is his body, the fulness of him that filleth all in all.

(Isaiah 40:22) *It is* he that sitteth upon the circle of the earth, and the inhabitants thereof *are* as grasshoppers; that stretcheth out the heavens as a curtain, and spreadeth them out as a tent to dwell in:

Obviously, He sits above the circle of the Earth. We understand that the earth is the Lord's and the fullness thereof – He is above. We are seated with him in heavenly places far above..., so understand that when you pray, you pray from that place. We pray from the place where we sit. We don't pray as someone defeated. The power of prayer is praying from where you sit. Where we sit is the place of authority.

Where we sit is the place of dominion. Understanding that place, the bible speaks concerning the right hand of God is power (Exodus 15:12), and also he sits at the father's right hand (1 Peter 3:22). So understanding the above, speaking from that place, walking in that place, commanding from that place is powerful, these are some of the things we must know. Understand that when you're praying as a believer, we have to come into a place where prayer moves from one dimension to another. You are sitting whilst worshipping in a quiet place and suddenly you began to stand and walk about. That means there is a dimension of warfare and authority that you've walked into which changed your posture for war. Immediately you see yourself releasing the decrees of God from the heavenly place.

I love this scripture in Matthew 18 verse 18.

Matthew 18 verse 18 says, whatsoever you bind on Earth shall be bound in heaven whatsoever. You loose on Earth shall be loosed in heaven. So what you do in that God dimension is suddenly exposed to that place of authority and dominion unto your praying.

Young Hearted

(Matthew 18:3) And said, Verily I say unto you, Except ye be converted, and become as little children, ye shall not enter into the Kingdom of heaven.

Humility is needed and a must when we approach ABBA Father God, as we can also see reflected in 2 chronicles 7:14

(2Ch 7:14) If my people, which are called by my name, shall humble themselves, and pray, and seek my face, and turn from their wicked ways; then will I hear from heaven, and will forgive their sin, and will heal their land.

We can see that there is a humbling and turning from wicked ways, a similar occurrence in the book of Jonah with the city of Nineveh. The people turned and repented from their evil ways, praying, fasting, and giving their lives to God (Jonah 3:6-9). So this brings us into a dimension of hope, satisfaction, increase and power.

Expectation

(Pro 23:18) For surely there is an end; and thine expectation shall not be cut off.

There must be anticipation, hope, and belief when we pray. This is where faith is in operation, as there must be an expectation. So when we pray, we have to possess that looking forward to, that's the believing dimension. We also begin to engage when we expect, we engage with the responsibility. When we engage, we will realise that we are not afraid when we want to ask God again.

Remembrance

(Isa 43:26) Put me in remembrance: let us plead together: declare thou, that thou mayest be justified.

The fact that you have prayed once does not mean that you cannot remind God, as God is the one that says put me in remembrance. Therefore you can remind and remember God in the place of prayer according to his word. This can be done either in Thanksgiving or Praise in advance of His promises. When we pray, that is when we get an effective prayer life, especially according to the word of God. So you can bring God's word back to him by saying, Father, according to your word you promised, then make your petition known to the Lord. The scripture cannot be broken, and you will see the hand of God like never before. Know that God's word NEVER returns unanswered!

(Isaiah 55:11) So shall my word be that goeth forth out of my mouth: it shall not return unto me void, but it shall accomplish that which I please, and it shall prosper in the thing whereto I sent it.

Prayer Altars
Set my prayer altar on fire

Prayer gives us the edge, and demons are afraid of the prayer place. The altar of prayer is a place of death to the flesh, longing for the Spirit, warfare and a fireplace. Until we conform to the burning bush, we cannot confront Pharoah. The part of building a prayer altar requires a sacrificial yes to God. When we say yes, we die on the altar waiting to carry His flames.

Hebrew 1:7 says he makes his ministers flames of fire. When we pray, fires are set up on our altar, and we must become a burning altar to dismantle other wicked altars. Remembering that we wrestle not against flesh and blood, but against principalities and power, so when we pray, we make our house an address in the realm of the spirit. When we pray, demons recognise that this person in this house is a no-go zone because they are prayerful. Satan and his demons are afraid of a prayerful person. This is why the devil comes against churches and people that pray. You are not only a lighthouse, you give others light by freeing men and women from the darkness.

"Prayer comes with grace and capacity the more you pray, so start! "

Our engagement in prayers provokes change. So the life of prayer is a necessity that we must cultivate; we must build the altar of prayer, as Isaiah says (see Isaiah 19:19-20) and become a living and burning altar, contending with family altars that have been there for decades or centuries. Therefore, short prayers have their place, as well as long prayers. When we build altars, we come to the knowledge or symbol of death and sacrifice at the altar. We lay down our lives and say no flesh would prevail only the spirit will prevail.

The altar of prayer is imperative in this world of warfare. We must sort this fight ourselves so that we no longer allow distraction and flesh to pull us out of our posture. It takes focus to build, the altar goes beyond stagnation and statuette, it moves. We can become a living altar moving around, and this is when prayer is a spirit. Prayer leaves a place like your Church building or room and follows you into the car, workplace, parks, bathrooms etc, this is the spirit of prayer. Everywhere you go, it becomes a part of you; that is why you can go pray somewhere and when you leave, you remember your encounter there, and it stirs a similar experience of prayer because it followed you. The atmosphere is not just in your room, it is in you now. You have become a living host of His presence wherever you go with the burning fire of prayer that people see the results.

We pray effectively, the more we pray, the more we increase, and greater our utterances. The solidification of our Prayer altar gives us stamina over demonic altars. We have foundational, family, personal or ancestral altars. We also have witchcraft and territorial altars. If you are not praying for your future, something or someone will stand in your way.

(Isaiah 6:1) In the year that King Uzziah died I saw the Lord sitting upon a throne, high and lifted up; and the train of his robe filled the temple.

King Uzziah was a system of an altar that blocks sight, until he died, Isaiah could not see beyond the now, the beauty of the Lord was not in manifestation. In this kind of case, it is altar versus altar. Every stubborn problem requires a rugged prayer life. So God is calling us again to raise the altar of prayer, houses of prayer and places of intimacy.

Prayer altars require holiness, orderliness, and purity of heart. Elijah raised an altar before calling on God (1 Kings 18:31-38). Put order back in your life. A double-minded person cannot build effectively or focus.

We want to see the Kingdom come and the power of God invade as we become a burning altar everywhere we go. I believe the mantle of prayer is upon this generation again, we will begin to see a resurgence of prayer in our churches, streets, campuses and houses again. We'll begin to see the effect of the engine House on every believer coming to fullness. Prayer is a necessity for us, we will see the altar of prayer burn once again. No more quietness, no more lukewarmness. I decree that the fire of your altar will not be extinguished in Jesus Name! Amen.

THE EFFECT OF PRAYER
WHY WE PRAY

As we explore the effectiveness of prayer and the power of prayer, we will begin to see a resurgence of prayers with results. God is not an antic prayer collector, He answers our prayers.

(Jeremiah 33:3) Call to me and I will answer you, and will tell you great and hidden things that you have not known.

Right from the Garden of Eden, God had a conversation with Adam, which can be read from the book of Genesis 2:3; 3:1-8 after we see that Adam and Eve fell by conversing with the Serpent. The Bible says Adam heard the voice of God as He came with a sound. That means there was an interaction and a conversation right from creation when God told him to name the animals. When we begin to consider prayer again, we will begin to come into the place of communication.

"Prayer is a communication and our right to God's Heart"

Believers have been communicating with different things and have lost their place. When the woman (Eve) began communicating with the serpent instead of God, it led them to act fleshly, and the glory was taken. That means when we leave the place of prayer, we leave the place of power. Prayer is the engine house of our spiritual walk. A believer moving without a prayer life is like a car without an engine. The car is in shape and has a steering wheel, but there is no engine. I believe the father is calling us back to prayer, and even in this book, the Lord will begin to ignite you again. There will be an ignition of prayer fire in us.

The Bible speak concerning a man called Elijah; it says Elijah was a man like us, just like the book of *James 5:19* speaks about him, he prayed earnestly. Prayer will force things to begin to happen.

....

"Prayer is a CALL to ALL. Not for the elites or leaders only."

....

We must understand that prayer is a necessity when it comes to living. Prayer is not a suggestion for every believer. *Men ought always*, and it's not an opinion. *Men ought always to pray and not to faint.* Luke 18:1. It must become a lifestyle that we cultivate the act of prayer as our daily food and our daily act. When we communicate with God, we see the expression of heaven. When we communicate with God, we see the advancement of heaven. When we communicate with God, we reflect the heart of God. So, prayer is mandatory for all.

"Prayer is asking NOT begging"
(Matthew 7:7)

Often time believers pray needy prayers. Prayer is not the satisfaction of our needs only. Yes! God supplies our needs in prayer, but a needy prayer is not effective. A lifestyle of prayer is an effective prayer. It brings us to an effective life because we are engaged daily.

Prayer is not a needy thing. Because we need a certain thing, we then go into prayer, and that is only when we pray. Men should always pray, not pray when there's a need to pray. No! *Men ought always to pray* is our identity. In the book of Luke 11:2, Jesus says that when you pray, "when" is mandatory and necessary for every believer.

"Prayer is not only receiving, but it is also giving, requires time and focus."

....

Jesus says, *when you pray*, this means a life of prayer must be the act of the believer. Prayer must be the living organism that flows in us continuously for advancement, increase, and the next dimension. It is a necessity when we pray, a necessity for what God is calling us to do.

PRAYER TRAVAIL FOR BREAKTHROUGH

Every travail is to birth the mind of the Spirit into existence. The push of something that is unique. When it comes to travail, the Bible interpret it to us as a woman in childbirth. When a woman is in childbirth, there is labouring and a pushing experience in action. The Bible says that Jacob came to a place where he travailed for his destiny and his life. We see from Genesis 32:24-28, a man who came to the place where he wrestled and fought. He came to the place where he said, God, you have to change me, there has to be a birthing of a new me from Jacob which means a trickster, and he was changed to become Israel.

We see the process of travailing, and the Bible says there was no time he left the angel of the Lord, he wrestled all through the night till the day break that the angel had to touch the socket of his hip to wrench for a release. After that, He was able to transform him and spoke a word over him, *what is the name?* And he said, "Your name shall no longer be called Jacob, but Israel; for you have struggled with God and with men, and have prevailed."

We see that a dimension of a travail leads to a prevailing moment. As a believer, many people want to birth something without understanding that it must first be birth out in a secret place. Travail is a moment of pushing, it's a moment of pain between our now and the next. I called travail a transition season of our life. Often, people tell me that God asked me to leave, God asked me to do certain things, but the moment between the now and that destination is called transition.

The in-between is not leaving, that middle is called in-between where travail breaks out, and that is called transition. That is the travailing moment. Many people fail at this junction when they do not know what to do. They are in the season of travail. They are in the season of contraction, and they have to push because when a labouring woman is in that place, fully dilated, you have to push out because there is a push pain between your transition stage and the next.

For every intercession and every prayer, there is that travail that comes. If God has called you, you must learn to travail in prayer, pushing, and posture until you see a breakthrough. You will not know the art of prevailing until you learn the art of travailing.

The act of travailing will lead you to prevail because the pain experience is going to lead to your joy experience.

The child's pain experience, according to "strong", is something that is called a pain of parturition, which is travail in birth. We know by definition that parturition is the act of giving birth. If we insert the meaning of travail into apostle Paul's statements (Gal 4:19), we have this, my little children whom I am experiencing in pains of birth again until Christ be formed in you. Paul said in Galatians 4:19, *my little children, of whom I travail in birth again until Christ be formed in you.* Nothing just comes; there's a travailing moment that happens. Everybody wants to be a spiritual father and mother, but they must understand that you cannot just gain spiritual children and not cover them. There is a place where you cover, push them by prayer, and cover them. There is that travailing place that leads to a prevailing place. The travailing place that leads to the greatness of men. So, we must know as a believer that in travailing pain, you must forget who is around you and posture your knees. When a woman is in that place where she wants to give birth, she forgets about everything to birth her baby.

I remember my beautiful wife years ago when my son was coming, and she held my ring hand, and I was like, my hand and she gave me a look because she was in a painful moment to push that time. It's a fight for life because if you don't push that thing out, that thing you're carrying can kill you or die inside. There is that place of prayer that every believer and intercessor must cultivate, like where angels begin to ascend and descend because there is a reaction. He held on to the angel until he saw his name change.

As believers, every one of us must understand the place of travail. Your ministry and your assignment cannot be birthed first outside. It is first birthed on your knees. It is first birthed on the floor. It is first birthed when no one sees you. Many want to show the signs of their ministry without the signs of being wrenched. A wrenched person has been through a travailing journey of life. We see that man Jacob began to limp because his socket had been dislocated from travailing with the angel. The size of your travailing shows that there is a mark, a hollow that has been displaced, which means there is something that has formed you. They are your knees that have touched the ground, and that is a place of prayer.

We speak about older people like A A Allen, and Smith Wigglesworth, but we knew that these people had the place of prayer, the place of power, which is prayer. We want to talk about their experience, but yet we don't want to understand what it takes to move from the secret place. There is a travail for a breakthrough that happens there. Only if we can posture back again to the place of prayer, only if we can arise back to the place of wailing. We would see the prevailing hand of God. Demons will quit, and evil spirits will begin to run.

We will see effective ministry because you are tested in the place of prayer. The amount of your prayer life will determine how you will mount your mountains. Our prayer life cultivates the root for longevity, character, personality, and whom God has called us to be. In the secret place, that travailing place, the assignment, the vision, the business, whatever God has called us to will begin to come into effect. Let us learn the act of travailing to prevailing it in the place of prayer.

PRAYER OF JABEZ

THE TECHNOLOGY OF PRAYER

Many people do pray. What is prayer? Prayer is a conversation, intercourse. It is speaking to one that is superior. Prayer itself is a vehicle, and almost everybody does it. The Christians pray to their God Yahweh, the Muslims will seek their Allah or Mohammed, and where we see all the other false gods like voodoo, stones, river gods, thunder and so on people speak to in praying. We understand that prayer is necessary and powerful when it is communicated directly with the Universe's Creator, God. When we pray, we must know that we are praying to the superior God above every other god that people pray to.

"Wherever you pray to and from, you command power from that realm"

Knowing that we pray from the place where He has called us, the Bible says we are seated with Him in heavenly places, far above principalities and power.

(Ephesian 2:6) And hath raised *us* up together, and made *us* sit together in heavenly *places* in Christ Jesus:

Our prayer expression with God must be in communication where we now begin to understand that we are speaking with our Father, and it is not a monologue. There must be a conversation when He comes, and it is a dialogue. When we communicate with our father, a dialogue happens in prayer. God, Himself, hears us when we pray. Believers must understand authority. The devil is trying to distract us, so we do not know where we speak from. We must understand where we sit. Jesus Christ admonished them to say, when you pray, say *our Father, who art in heaven,* knowing that we speak from heaven, we do not pray to any other god. We meet people for assistance, and we join together to pray. The Bible says if any man is sick, let him call the elder and let them pray, and the prayer of faith shall cause the sick person to be healed (James 5:14-16).

One of the things we must understand is that prayer causes things to change, prayer breaks protocol and prayer opens the door. Speaking from the dimension of where we sit with God, knowing that our Heavenly Father is in charge, causes us to walk in boldness and make us believe that there is a God that answers us. It's important to also note that whenever we pray like the unbelievers, flesh and emptiness are in manifestation. But when we pray knowing that we are praying to the creator of heaven and earth, He backs us. The Bible says the angel of the Lord encamps round about those that fear the Lord and deliver them (Palms 34:7).

When we pray, we know that there is an angelic manifestation that encamps about us. Knowing that Prayer is a powerful weapon for the believers is an authority that causes us to stand in the place where He has called us.

We must also understand that prayer is not for players.

"Prayer or praying is not a mistake for laziness – Prayer build, makes and shapes the future men and women"

Many people find themself in a crowd trying to make their voices loud. Prayer is not powerful when it's loud. Yes, there is a loud cry of prayer, the Bible says in (John 11:37-43) that Jesus Christ wept because He heard about the death of Lazarus, and we see He came in and cried with a loud voice of prayer. There is a loud voice of prayer and that is a time when we say enough is enough. We must also know that prayer is not about the mouth, boosting or a trick to make people come around us and say, yes, they are praying. We don't see the result because people's mouths and hearts are not aligning in the place of prayer. Until our heart, mouth, and posture are synchronised, we will not see the effectiveness of prayer.

Jesus Christ cried out, come forth, Lazarus. That is a loud cry. To close your mouth when you are supposed to shout is a death sentence to your future.

OPERATION JABEZ

The same principle to Jabez. The Bible says Jabez was more honourable, and he prayed.

(1Chronicle 4:9-10) Now Jabez was more honorable than his brothers, and his mother called his name [a]Jabez, saying, "Because I bore *him* in pain." **10** And Jabez called on the God of Israel saying, "Oh, that You would bless me indeed, and enlarge my [b]territory, that Your hand would be with me, and that You would keep *me* from evil, that I may not cause pain!" So God granted him what he requested.

"Marrying your enough with God's word concerning you provokes a shout for change".

He came to a place where he cried; enough is enough. The reason why we see the enemy oppressing us, the reason we see the enemy gaining ground, is because we don't have a people of prayer, and it's time to rise back to prayer. It's time for the altar of prayer to be ignited again in our homes, street, churches, and hubs. God is raising the movement of people that will pray. This is not just a building, people will pray in the street, people we pray at all times. The Bible says *pray without ceasing.* Praying without ceasing causes us to pray when we are walking; when we are sitting, we are praying. We do not need to be in the house to maintain a prayer life.

You can be anywhere, and the God you call will show forth. We must also understand that you get the spiritual antenna in some places. This was the mystery of Jacob, and the Bible says Jacob, when he came to a place, he found that the angels were ascending and descending there. There was a magnetic principle in that place because of his grandfather Abraham who prayed there (Genesis 12), and we see that when Jacob got to the place, he prayed. Prayer must come back to our churches. Prayer without ceasing is a lifestyle. We pray without allowing the workplace to define our walk with Jesus. When the Holy Spirit is in charge, praying in tongues everywhere loud and in silence. You're driving; you're praying. Your car can become a place of your altar where you pray. If it is not working in your house because it's crowded, get into your car or take a walk around. Wherever you make a place of prayer, become a place of power. So, it is time for us to rise up and pray because God is calling us to awake to the place of prayer.

———————

"Wherever you make a place of prayer,

become a place of power"

———————

PASSION FOR PRAYER

The passion for prayer is an expression of a deeper dimension of God. A craving begins to explode in your belly for a deeper walk. This is the belly dimension, and I believe God is placing a passion within you. Passion for God is uncontrollable Jeremiah says:

(Jeremiah 20:9)Then I said, "I will not make mention of Him, nor speak any more in His name." But His word was in mine heart as a burning fire shut up in my bones; and I was weary with forbearing, and I could not hold back

A drive begins to cause your place of religiosity to begin to get dissatisfied. When you get tired of religion, just going to church, it's a passion, a hunger that is being formed in your heart. The book of Acts chapter 2 tells us that *"they were in the upper room, and they began to fellowship in one accord, and the Bible said they began to pray"*. That was a place for more, a place of the promise of the Father. When prayer becomes the place for more and the place of I want more, fire is released.

This is my story. Years ago, I was in the church, where I served in the leadership as a music director for over seven years. I will begin to worship God and begin to praise, and there was power in the place. I remember vividly that when I opened the door, I walked through the back of the church and began to walk down to my house, tears drips down my cheek in frustration because there was a yearning in my belly that was pulling me to the place of intimacy and I began to cry and say to God, Father, what is this? God began to say, Son, I want to pull you close to me, to the place of intimacy, to a dimension that flesh cannot enter, the place of hunger and encounters. I began to see the craving for more of God and the Holy Spirit.

I made sure that the place of intimacy that hunger was building until I had to say to my leader that I wanted to seek the face of God, I just wanted to be with God. Though he agreed, I could see from his expression that he was unhappy. From that moment, three weeks was the transforming moment of my life. A week became two weeks, two weeks became three weeks, and after the third week, it became a lifestyle that I began to fast and seek the face of God for nearly a whole year. There is a passion that God is causing to rise up in the church, now in the believers.

"The craving within is pulling you to the original you before the foundation"

The reason you are craving, the reason you're saying, 'God, I'm dissatisfied' is because God wants to bring you into the place of intimacy where you become an altar that is moving with fire. Jesus told them, tarry here until you are empowered (Luke 24:49). There is a fire coming to the body of Christ, to those who have learned the act of tarrying, the act of waiting, those who are not rushing out of the secret place, those who are not rushing out of the womb. If you can find a place, if you can find the posture of prayer, then you've found the place of power. I say to people always, cultivate the place of prayer, and men will look for you. Cultivate the secret place, keep praying, worshipping, waiting, and fasting. One day your voice will be heard. One day you will come up higher. Many people are pursuing and running after the pulpit, going after things; they just want to be known, but yet they do not know the secret place. It was in the upper room that the apostles and the disciples found themselves until the Holy Spirit came and rested on them, endue and transformed them. Transformation is done in the secret place. The hunger that is rising in you, the hunger and the passion that is crying out in your belly is divinity.

God is about to fill you, God is about to satisfy you so that no devil will be able to stand against you. You are going to rise in your family, and you are going to stand up because of this hunger. He is going to make break the curse, and you will be the barrier breaker. You will be the one in your family that will break the generational curse. That's why you must come into the place of prayer and identify with the God who is the lifter of your head. Your knees are about to be ignited again and strengthened for prayer like never before. God is going to strengthen your knees again. Your knees will no longer be weak because there are spirits that attack people from the place of prayer that causes men to become slumbered, that causes sleep to begin to come upon your eyes; I decree and declare this over you, that spirit is going to die today in the name of Jesus. The Bible says that Jesus Christ prayed and took Peter, and what happened? Peter said, the spirit is willing, but the flesh is weak (Matthew 26:41).

There are spirits in operation that have tried to give your flesh access to begin to see your flesh override the spiritual expression. I come against that spirit today in the name of Jesus, your spirit will gain muscles again. when we pray, what we do is build our spiritual muscles. It gives us the capacity; the more we pray with fasting, the more there is a momentum that will begin to rise, understanding that place and the passion of prayer. God is calling, causing it to ignite in your life again like never before. You will see yourself praying for 30 minutes, God is going to stretch you, and from 30 minutes, you're going to pray for 1 hour; from one hour, you will begin to find yourself.

I remember reading a book by a man of God in Africa years ago. When I read the book, there was a hunger in my belly that hit me so much for prayer. That is where I got the heartbeat of prayer. Immediately, I prayed for one hour after I dropped that book. As you're reading this book, that fire will light you up. There is a fire that is going to stretch your capacity. After that experience, weeks later, I remember first praying in tongues for five hours straight, and when I came out, I saw a witch running from the street. I remember a lady with an idol; her house was full of idols, and when I came, she ran. Why? That is when God began to say to me, Son, do you not know all that happened because of your prayer all through the night? I prayed from 12 midnight to 5 am, that was my first prayer in tongues.

God's capacity and strength came upon me the first time I prayed, and that happened. That was a shift! The more you pray, the more the hunger intensifies, and the more you build capacity. Many people want to build capacity without tarrying long.

START HERE NOW!

I want you to start by praying for 5-10 minutes, 30 minutes, 40 minutes, and 1 hour. That is how you build the two hours, three hours to four hours in that place. There was a time I prayed in tongues for over eight hours from 8 pm, I started praying in tongues and got to 7 am the next day. There was also a time on August 6th - 8th 2022 on retreat when God placed me on the floor for 40 hours, three days Praying. Why? Because God began to do certain things that moment, He took time off my mind, and prayer got into my belly, and days became like hours, and I have seen the hand of God come upon me because the place of prayer has become a place of intimacy where the spirit communicate. When you cultivate that dimension because of the hunger in your belly, give the place to God. Give your heart to God and give that dimension to God, and begin to see God take you above your limit in the place of prayer. I pray that the Almighty God will begin to strengthen your life of prayer like never before in the name of Jesus.

PRAYERS AND DECLARATIONS

Prayers Against The Python Spirit.

By the power of the Almighty God, Lord Jesus, I come against the Python spirit that has been assigned to suffocate, tie down and squeeze the life out of the people of the children of God. The Python spirit has come to break them out of structure, out of place, out of position, and out of alignment in the place of prayer. We come against the Python spirit that is squeezing you, muzzling you, muscling your mouth, so that your mouth will be open once again. I decree and declare that your mouth will speak power, that your mouth will pray again, and your knees will be posture again. The Python spirit is destroyed. Father, according to Act 28:5, Paul shook the snake into the fire, father, but the fire of God, let every python spirit that has been assigned to mute us, to keep us stagnant, to keep us not to be able to pray, we come against that spirit, in the name of Jesus. Now, be free, be unmuted to move, to excel, to pray and to advance in Jesus' name.

Prayer Against Engine Killers

Father, we thank you because we know that prayer is the engine of every believer, for your word says, Men ought always to pray and not to faint. By the fire of God, we contend against every engine killer, the spirit that has been assigned to kill our prayer alter, father, we break that spirit, we contend against that spirit, in the name of Jesus, the spirit assigned to take us out of the place of prayer so they can affect our home, school, ministry and health, father, we destroy the Spirit by the power of the Lord Jesus, in the name of Jesus. Every spirit assigned to take out our engine, we destroy the spirit in the powerful name of Jesus. We put our engine of prayer back into alignment. We put our engine of intercession back into alignment, that our voices will be heard again, that our voices will open up again, and no spirit will be able to mute us and keep us bound. Lord Jesus, I come against that spirit that would try to destroy us that would try to destroy our engines in the church. We break it today. We lose that spirit today in the name of Jesus. Amen

Arise To Prayer Declarations.

Father, I decree and declare that the hand of God will begin to arise again over you, that no longer shall the place of prayer become the place where things have become cold. I decree and declare over your life that the hand and the manifestation of the Father will pull you off look warmness. I decree and declare, the father says Men ought always to pray and not to faint, you will not faint in the name of Jesus. The spirit of fainting will no longer be found in your camp. I decree and declare that everything that causes us to faint in the place of prayer, die in the name of

Jesus. Everything called stagnation, I decree and I declare, die in the name of Jesus. I pray, my father, my maker, I declare and break the spirit of stagnation, the spirit of slumber, the spirit of sleep that causes men to sleep through the night even when their father wakes them up to pray. I break that spirit in the name of Jesus Christ.

Father, insert a greater dimension and hunger for prayer in us again. Insert in us the capacity and the drive for prayer like never before. Father, we refuse to be defeated in the place of prayer. Once again, Lord, let your hand rest upon us. We arise and pray. We arise and war, we arise to overcome, we arise to take back again in the place of prayer, in the name of Jesus. Father, show forth your glory because you make your ministers flames of fire according to Hebrews 1:7, set us on fire once again. Lord, I decree, on fire, we will be, we arise once again in the name of Jesus. Amen.

Printed in Great Britain
by Amazon

19246138R00066